Life in a Medieval Castle and Village Coloring Book

by

JOHN GREEN

DOVER PUBLICATIONS, INC., NEW YORK

Illustrations copyright © 1990 by John Green.
Text copyright © 1990 by Dover Publications, Inc.
All rights reserved under Pan American and International Copyright Conventions.

Published in Canada by General Publishing Company, Ltd., 30 Lesmill Road, Don Mills, Toronto, Ontario.
Published in the United Kingdom by Constable and Company, Ltd., 3 The Lanchesters, 162–164 Fulham Palace Road, London W6 9ER.

Life in a Medieval Castle and Village Coloring Book is a new work, first published by Dover Publications, Inc., in 1990.

DOVER *Pictorial Archive* SERIES

International Standard Book Number: 0-486-26542-0

Manufactured in the United States of America
Dover Publications, Inc., 31 East 2nd Street, Mineola, N.Y. 11501

Introduction

For the sake of convenience, the Middle Ages are generally thought of as beginning with the fall of the Roman Empire of the West in the fifth century and continuing through to about 1500, when the rediscovery of the Classical tradition, voyages of discovery, recovery of widespread international trade and communications, the introduction of printing and the Reformation produced profound changes in society. The dates, however, are far from absolute. Although the early Middle Ages were marked by the almost complete collapse of urban life in Northern Europe, the decline can be seen as having begun in the later years of the Roman Empire; the roots of what became the feudal system can be traced to the management of some of the great Roman estates.

The absence of Roman administration affected all aspects of life: large-scale trade and commerce almost ceased, manufactures declined precipitously, civil government was often lacking. The Church itself, which had become the state religion of the empire, almost succumbed under the relentless pounding of the invasions of the barbarians, finding refuge in Ireland and some of the Scottish isles. But order was restored gradually, and a fusion of the elements retained from Rome with the customs brought by the Germanic peoples created a new society.

The Middle Ages, spanning a thousand years, were hardly static. The resumption of travel and trade, the rise of the merchant class and the havoc wrought by war, famine and plague were constantly changing Europe. Conditions and customs varied greatly from area to area and year to year. This book gives a general picture of life in the Middle Ages as it was lived in castle, village and town.

After the fall of the Roman Empire of the West, defense became the major concern of communities. Villages such as the one in the foreground were rarely far from a castle or, as shown here, a fortified town where refuge could be taken in times of danger. Walled cities such as Carcassonne, Avignon, York and Aigues-Mortes still exist.

1

The economy was primarily agricultural. The soil was tilled by serfs—peasants who were bound to the land and enjoyed very little freedom. The local lord granted them land and protection; they were obliged to perform many duties and services for him. The practice of agriculture was laborious and, by modern standards, extremely inefficient.

2

Among the lord's dues were fixed amounts of a serf's produce. Sometimes the amount could be paid in coin. The local lord, in turn, owed allegiance to a mightier noble who had sworn fealty to the king. This rigid hierarchy was the backbone of feudalism.

The size and elaborateness of castles varied greatly. This is a very complex castle, with moat and drawbridge. The banner at the right waves over the turret of the keep. The stronger a castle was, the greater threat it posed to central authority in a kingdom. Castles such as Caernarvon, Caerphilly and Conway in Wales and Chillon in Switzerland still dominate the landscape.

Successful defense depended on more than stout walls. In great castles, armories produced the armor worn by knights. At first armor consisted of chain mail (some of which lies on the table, to the right). Gradually, armor made of large plates covering the entire body was developed. It was extremely expensive, and only elite knights could wear it.

5

A good suit of armor had to be made to measure. Helping arm the knight was no mean feat; after undergarments had been put on, the suit of armor had to be donned in a specific order. Frequently the armorer was present to make any last-minute "alterations." With the development of accurate artillery and the shift from hand-to-hand combat between knights to encounters between large forces of foot soldiers, the wearing of armor was relegated to ceremonial occasions. The suits were so elaborately decorated that they were works of art in themselves.

The keep of the castle was the highest point and the center of defense. In the absence of a central authority, defenses were local, and the responsibility of the lord. At times of danger, a signal was sounded to warn people in the area so they could seek protection within the castle.

Warfare was brutal, battles tending to be brief but intense. Although an armed knight was almost invincible when mounted, weapons such as the halberd (held by the foot soldier at the left) had a hook at the end that could be used to pull the knight from his horse. On the ground, he could be killed. Another effective weapon against armor was the longbow, measuring six feet in length. Requiring 100 pounds of draw, it could fire six arrows a minute and

had an effective range of 100 yards. Favored by the English, it proved its superiority to the crossbow at the battles of Crécy (1346), Poitiers (1356) and Agincourt (1415) in the Hundred Years' War. The shields of the knights are painted with their coats of arms. Initially intended simply to identify the individual, the designs became regulated by elaborate rules of heraldry to reflect the bearer's ancestry and position in his family.

The machinery of warfare was primitive. On the right, a catapult (also called a mangonel or onager) hurls a rock against the castle walls. Behind it is a movable tower. On top, protected by a roof, are soldiers who will try to cross over to the castle when it is pushed against the walls. Other methods of attack included sapping—digging tunnels to undermine the walls—and the use of battering rams.

Once the outer defenses were breached, attacking forces were faced with interior walls, the keep being the final line of defense. In the background, defending forces use Greek fire, an inflammable composition that was ignited and poured on attackers below. Cannon was developed in the fifteenth century. Able to reduce walls to rubble in little time, artillery revolutionized warfare. The castle as a means of defense became obsolete.

The development of the skills needed in warfare was a full-time occupation. While arm-to-arm combat is practiced with wooden swords on the left, a knight tilts at a shield mounted with a counterbalance.

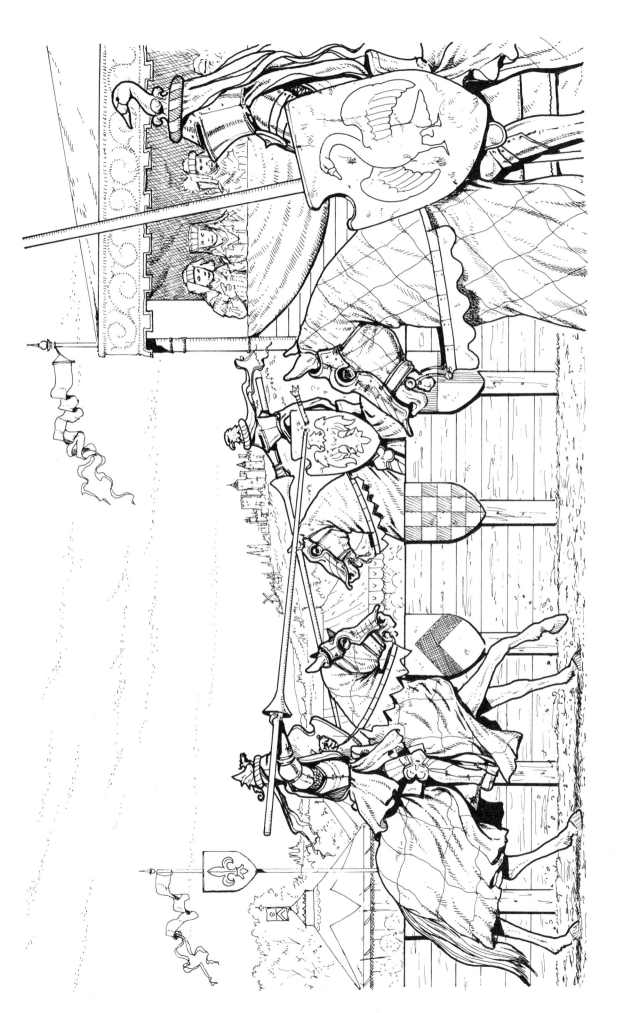

Great tournaments allowed knights to display their skill and courage before an audience. Originating as mêlées—mock battles that had alarmingly high mortality rates—these displays evolved into safer, better-regulated forms, such as the jousting seen here. Although tournaments became increasingly formal and ceremonial, Henri II of France was killed during a joust in 1559.

Archery was a skill needed for defense and hunting. While the boy in the foreground receives instruction in handling the bow, archers behind him take aim at butts.

Although the gun, developed in the fifteenth century, replaced the bow and arrow, archery remains popular as a sport.

14

Hunting was a favorite pastime of the aristocracy, hunting rights being jealously guarded by local lords. In the background, a stag flees hunters and a pack of dogs. In the foreground, the lord practices falconry—hunting with a falcon or hawk. The bird on his wrist is ready to fly after its prey and bring it to earth. The bird on the attendant's wrist wears its jesses (leather thongs attached to its legs) and a soft leather hood. The type of bird used was prescribed by the owner's social status.

15

There was a gentler side to life in the castle in the Middle Ages. Within its walls, herb gardens were tended for food and medicinal purposes. The beehives in the background provide honey (sugar was a great luxury); pigeons (a source of food) nest in the dovecot at the top of the tower. In·Aquitaine and Provence in France, there grew a tradition of courtly love, praised by troubadours, that turned the relationship between a lady and her lover into a ritual. A knight's conduct in love and war was regulated by the codes of chivalry, which reached their height in the thirteenth and fourteenth centuries.

The lady of the castle sits for her toilette while a nurse tends her child. Although women were accorded few rights during the Middle Ages, the period was influenced by some who made a lasting mark on history, including Queen Margaret of Denmark, Eleanor of Aquitaine, Blanche of Castile and Margaret of Anjou.

Early in the Middle Ages, nobles and their dependents lived in a common area; later they withdrew to privacy in their own quarters. The lady of the castle is busy with her needlework (considered an important accomplishment) as she is serenaded by a musician playing an early stringed instrument. The lord and his son play chess. A tapestry hung on the wall covers the door, cutting down drafts.

On special occasions, such as Christmas, the lord of the castle gave a feast or series of feasts in the Great Hall. Enjoying the entertainment provided by the juggler and by the musician playing an early cittern, the ranking members of the castle sit on the dais, the others below.

Food was served in great quantity and frequently featured dishes more notable for their exotic appeal—such as peacock—and for their elaborate preparation than for their taste.

Cooks prepare a banquet in the huge castle kitchens. Meat is turning on the spit over the fire while a cauldron bubbles alongside. In the days before refrigeration, the greatest variety of food was had during the warm months. A cook had to be resourceful during the winter. Although spices were rare and expensive, they were frequently used heavily to disguise the taste of meat that had spoiled.

Another section of the castle was the bakehouse, where bread, one of the most important staples, was made in great ovens. Most villages had a bakehouse, owned by the lord, that sold bread to the villagers. Baking was one of the many skills that suffered an eclipse during the early Middle Ages. By the thirteenth century, however, the art was being revived by guilds.

In contrast to the home of his lord, the home of a serf was much less grand. Houses such as this were made of timber frame and wattle-and-daub construction.

The interior of a serf's house was equally simple. Of one or two rooms, its interior was shared by livestock. The smoke from the open hearth was vented through a hole cut in the roof. Household goods were few and simple, utensils being of wood and pottery, with some metal. The diet was limited and monotonous.

Certain services were needed in a castle or village. Farriers (blacksmiths) were vital to the maintenance of horses. The skill had been introduced to the British Isles by William the Conqueror.

Most cloth produced in Europe during the Middle Ages was made of wool. In a single peasant household, it was possible to carry out all the steps in the manufacture of textiles: cleaning, carding, spinning, weaving, shearing off knots and dyeing. The cloth, however, was coarse; for better material, weaving was done by skilled artisans.

Sheep provided wool, meat and milk. Shepherds were expected to be with their flocks at all times. At some periods, raising sheep became so profitable and widespread that it threatened to take over agricultural land for pasturage.

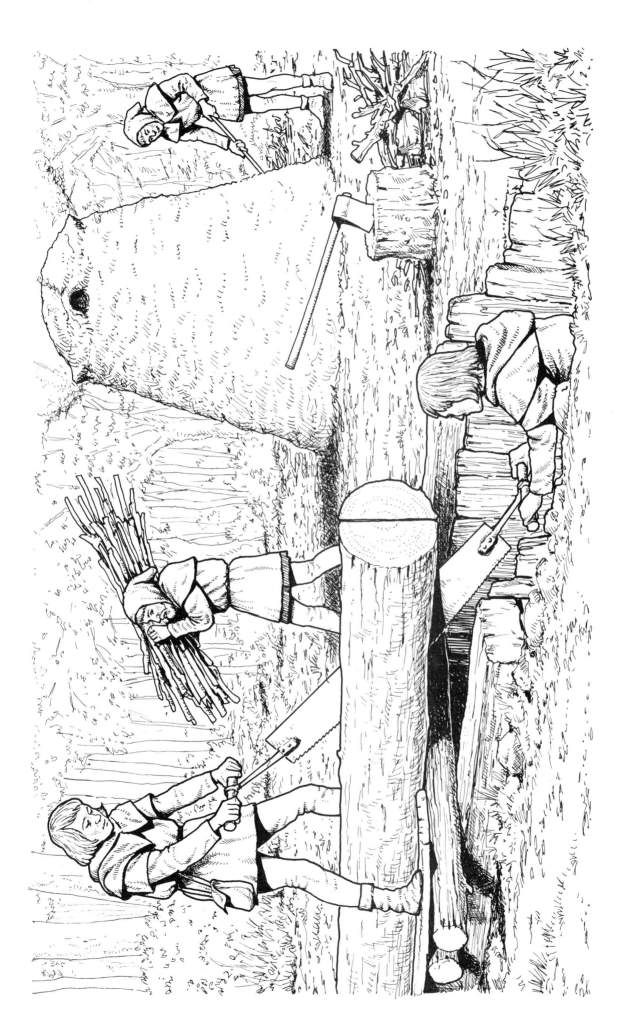

Much of Europe was covered with dense forest that supplied timber. Regulation of its uses was in the hands of the local lord, who accorded various rights to his peasants. The two men working in the saw pit prepare wood for building. In the rear, a serf makes charcoal in an earth oven. Yet another serf is gathering firewood.

Grain was ground into flour at the mill. An independent miller kept a certain amount of the grain milled as his fee. If the mill belonged to a lord, his serfs were obliged to use it and, frequently, to give a very large percentage of the flour to the lord. Wind- and water-powered mills were among the technological innovations of the Middle Ages.

At the beginning of the Middle Ages, towns had become little more than armed camps. Gradually they recovered and took on a life that was distinct from village or country; as centers of commerce and manufacturing, they were less encumbered by feudal bonds.

As the focal point of a town's life, the market was usually located at the geographic center. Here free farmers (and serfs with a surplus to sell) brought their produce. Other

goods were also displayed, variety increasing as trade
was reestablished.

Taverns provided those away from home with a means of eating. In many, meat was cooked and sold to be eaten away from the premises. As inns, they provided a stopping place for merchants and other travelers. In early days, the innkeeper was associated with the marketplace and helped accommodate visiting merchants.

Different aspects of village life come together at the stream. The boy on the left shows his mother fish he has caught as she takes buckets of water to the house (which does not have running water). In the background, a scold (a nagging woman) is being punished by being ducked.

For minor offenses, criminals were punished at the stocks (background) or pillory (foreground). Medieval justice, meted out by the aristocracy and Church, was frequently not so lenient. Torture was practiced and capital punishment was prescribed for many crimes. Heavy fines could be levied and bribery was widespread.

34

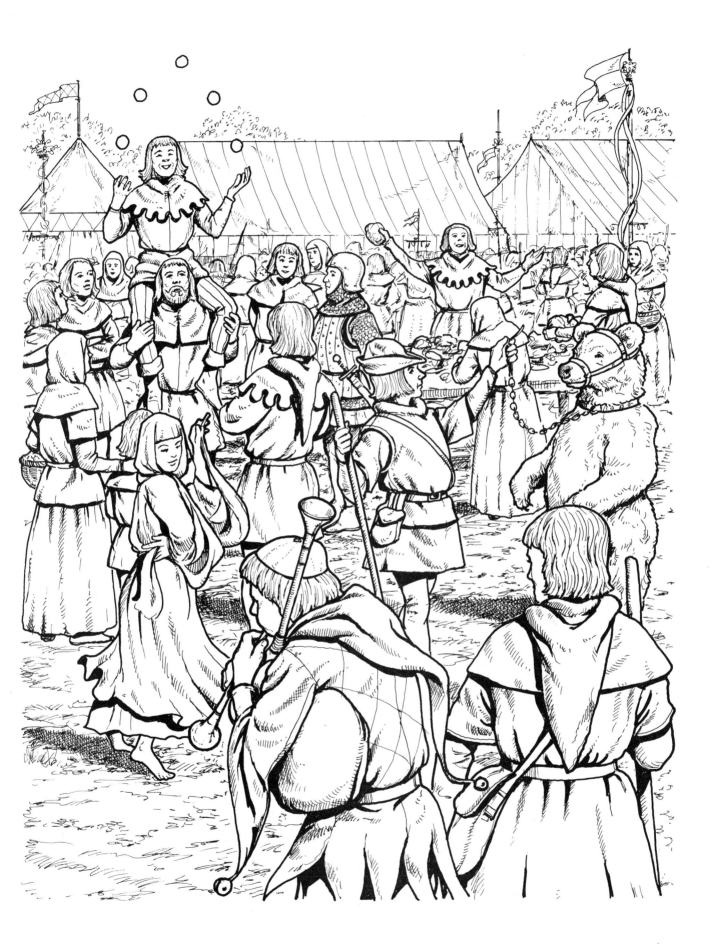

Fairs were held annually. In the early Middle Ages, they were important for the trade they attracted, and merchants attended when they could. Later, fairs were marked more by the diversity of entertainment they offered, and prefigured the modern circus.

Monks go to prayer in a monastery. The Church was the most powerful force in the Middle Ages, having assumed many of the functions that had previously been filled by the Roman government. Although its holdings of land were enormous, they were not subject to taxation by the secular government. The struggle between the Church and state was frequently bitter.

The Church raised many great structures that survive to this day, including the cathedrals of Notre Dame (Paris), Chartres, Canterbury, Rheims and Milan. The Middle Ages developed its own architectural styles—first the Romanesque, then the Gothic. Construction was super-vised by a master mason who acted as architect and administrator. The skilled men under his supervision—masons, glaziers, carpenters and the like—frequently came from guilds and received wages for their work.

The Church was the great instrument for the transmission of knowledge. The ability to read and write had
almost disappeared (Edward III, for example, was func-
tionally illiterate) but, in the thirteenth century, a
literate laity, taught by the Church, began to emerge.
Literacy was needed by the rising merchant class to carry
on its business.

A monk copies a book in the scriptorium of a monastery. The Church was also responsible for the preservation and transmission of the written word. The scribes' work saved many documents dating from classical antiquity, and chronicles and annals by such writers as the Vener-able Bede provide us with much of the knowledge we have of medieval history. The calligraphy of the monks still influences calligraphic styles today. Many of the books, also featuring exquisite illuminations, are great works of art.

As an act of penitence, or to supplicate for better health, people went on pilgrimages. The most important sites of pilgrimage were the Holy Land and Rome, but Santiago de Compostela in Spain and Canterbury in England were other major sites. The poor treatment of pilgrims in the Holy Land at the hand of the Muslims offered the pretext for the Crusades, which transformed the medieval world. Geoffrey Chaucer (ca. 1342–1400) immortalized a band of pilgrims in his *Canterbury Tales*.

Peddlers went from town to town and village to village, plying their wares. They also acted as a means of disseminating news, communications having deteriorated when the excellent system of Roman roads fell into decay. News spread very slowly, and frequently became garbled and confused.

Technological advances included innovations in ship-
ping. Vessels were decked over, many relied entirely on
sail (as opposed to those manned at oars), "castles" were
added to stern and bow. The magnetic compass, a boon to
navigation, was also introduced.

On the Mediterranean, merchants were hampered by Arab domination and the threat of pirates. The Venetians, in part, founded their prosperity on their ability to transport goods from Mediterranean ports in Africa and the Levant to Europe. But increased trade also facilitated the devastation of the Black Death (1347–51), a plague that spread throughout Europe from port cities, killing a third of the population. With the resultant scarcity of labor, more people were able to work for wages, weakening the feudal system.

The rise of the merchant class heralded the end of the Middle Ages. Italian merchants created banking, which greatly aided trade. Voyages of discovery and the discovery of the New World threw the emphasis of trade outside the Mediterranean, ending Venetian hegemony.

The invention of movable type and the printed book helped to create an explosion in learning. By the middle of the sixteenth century, the world and the way it looked at itself had changed beyond recognition.